This poetry book belongs to

. . . .

OXFORD
UNIVERSITY PRESS

Great Clarendon Street, Oxford OX2 6DP, United Kingdom

Oxford University Press is a department of the University of Oxford.
It furthers the University's objective of excellence in research,
scholarship, and education by publishing worldwide

Oxford is a registered trade mark of Oxford University Press
in the UK and in certain other countries

This selection and arrangement © John Foster 2016
Illustrations © Oxford University Press 2007

Illustrations by: Graham Round, Andy Cooke, Jane Gedye, Jan Lewis, Lynda Murray,
Merida Woodford, Denise Lindsay, Bucket, Renée Williams, Ann Johns, Fiona Dunbar,
Paul Dowling, Sally Kilroy, Jane Bottomley, Jessica Thomson, Claire Pound, Jenny
Williams, Yajia Gao, Samantha Rugen, Mary Griese, David Holmes, Martin Ursell.

Cover illustration by: Bestujeva Sofya/Shutterstock

The moral rights of the author/illustrator have been asserted
Database right Oxford University Press (maker)

First published in 2016

British Library Cataloguing in Publication Data
Data available

978-0-19-274470-8

10 9 8 7 6 5 4 3 2 1

Printed in China

Paper used in the production of this book is a natural, recyclable product made
from wood grown in sustainable forests.The manufacturing process conforms to
the environmental regulations of the country of origin.

Although we have made every effort to trace and contact all copyright holders before
publication this has not been possible in all cases. If notified, the publisher will rectify
any errors or omissions at the earliest opportunity.

Links to third party websites are provided by Oxford in good faith and for information
only. Oxford disclaims any responsibility for the materials contained in any third party
website referenced in this work.

I Can Read!
Oxford Poetry

For 5 Year Olds

With foreword by
Series Editor, John Foster

OXFORD

Acknowledgements

We are grateful to the authors in each case unless otherwise stated, for permission to include their poems:

Marie Brookes, 'My Goldfish', first published in *Pet Poems* (OUP, 1991), © Marie Brookes 1991.

John Coldwell, 'When the Giant Comes to Breakfast', first published in *Food Poems* (OUP, 1991), and 'My Pet Giraffe', first published in *Pet Poems* (OUP, 1991) © John Coldwell 1991.

Gina Douthwaite, 'Milking Time', first published in *Farm Poems* (OUP, 1995), © Gina Douthwaite 1995.

Eric Finney, 'Wrong Trolley', first published in *Shopping Poems* (OUP, 1995), © Eric Finney 1995, reprinted by permission of Mrs Sheilagh Finney.

John Foster, 'I Like', 'I Went to the Fridge', 'When Susie's Eating Custard', 'Poppadoms', and 'Chinese Takeaway', first published in *Food Poems* (OUP, 1991), © John Foster 1991; 'Pancake Day', first published in *Special Days Poems* (OUP, 1991), © John Foster 1991; 'With My Hand' and 'I Am the Boss', first published in *Body Poems* (OUP, 1995), 'One Summer Evening', first published in *Seasons Poems* (OUP, 1995), © John Foster 1995; and 'Zoo Dream', first published in *Number Poems* (OUP, 1994), © John Foster 1994.

David Harmer, 'Picnic Tea', first published in *Food Poems* (OUP, 1991), © David Harmer 1991.

Julie Holder, 'Loud and Soft', first published in *Sounds Poems* (OUP, 1995), 'First Steps', first published in *Movement Poems* (OUP, 1995), 'Shopping List', first published in *Food Poems* (OUP, 1995), 'Seasons of Trees', first published in *Seasons Poems* (OUP, 1995), © Julie Holder 1995.

Richard James, 'My Machine', first published in *Sounds Poems* (OUP, 1995) and 'The Barn Owl', first published in *Farm Poems* (OUP, 1995), © Richard Edwards 1995.

Wendy Larmont, 'Winter Walk' first published in *Seasons Poems* (OUP, 1995), © Wendy Larmont 1995, and 'Chinese New Year', first published in *Special Days Poems* (OUP, 1991), © Wendy Larmont 1991.

Daphne Lister, 'The Wuzzy Wasps of Wasperton', first published in *Minibeasts Poems* (OUP, 1993), © Daphne Lister 1993; 'The Echo Bridge', first published in *Sounds Poems* (OUP, 1995) and 'Playthings', first published in *Movement Poems* (OUP, 1995), © Daphne Lister 1995.

Tony Mitton, 'My Big Band', first published in *Sounds Poems* (OUP, 1995), and 'Hibernating Hedgehog', first published in *Seasons Poems* (OUP, 1995), © Tony Mitton 1995, reprinted by permission of David Higham Associates.

Judith Nicholls, 'Can You Hear?', first published in *Sounds Poems* (OUP, 1995), and 'Whoops', first published in *Shopping Poems* (OUP, 1995), © Judith Nicholls 1995; 'Christmas Eve', first published in *Special Days Poems* (OUP, 1991), © Judith Nicholls 1991.

Marian Swinger, 'Bouncing to the Moon', first published in *Movement Poems* (OUP, 1995), © Marian Swinger 1995, and 'Eid Mubarak', first published in *Special Days Poems* (OUP, 1991), © Marian Swinger 1991.

Charles Thomson with John Foster, 'You Can Tell It's Spring' first published in *Seasons Poems* (OUP, 1995), © Charles Thomson and John Foster 1995.

Irene Yates, 'Bonfire Night' and 'At Bimla's House Last Night' first published in *Special Days Poems* (OUP, 1991), © Irene Yates 1991.

Although we have made every effort to trace and contact all copyright holders before publication this has not been possible in all cases. If notified, the publisher will rectify any errors or omissions at the earliest opportunity.

Welcome!

This book provides a selection of poems to share with your child, which will help them become more confident with their reading. Children whose parents read with them at home and talk about what they read have a huge advantage at school.

The National Curriculum stresses the importance of children enjoying a variety of literary forms, not just stories. This includes an emphasis on reading and understanding poetry through learning, performing and reciting it. By Year 3 children should also be able to identify themes and express views.

When you read with your child, not only do they develop their reading skills, they also learn that reading is a pleasurable activity. By reading and discussing poems together you can begin to foster an enjoyment of poetry that will extend beyond their schooldays.

As well as providing a lively collection of poems for you to share, this book contains practical tips on how to introduce the poems and suggestions of activities you can use after reading, such as how to prepare a performance.

I can remember sharing nursery rhymes and poems with my parents and with my own children. The shared experience of listening to and joining in with reciting poems is one of the reasons I started writing children's poetry. From an early age I developed an interest in the sound of words and how you could play with them to make up rhymes.

I have been lucky enough to be invited to put together collections of my own and other people's poems for you to share and enjoy with your child. I hope you will have as much fun reading and performing them together as I did choosing them.

John Foster

Contents

Parent notes 8

My Goldfish is the Perfect Pet

My Goldfish *by Marie Brooks* 14

Pets *by Gwenda Izzet* 16

Zoo Dream *by John Foster* 20

In My Garden *by Gwenda Izzet* 24

The Wuzzy Wasps of Wasperton *by Daphne Lister* ... 26

My Pet Giraffe *by John Coldwell* 28

Ting! Went the Triangle

My Big Band *by Tony Mitton* 30

My Machine *by Richard James* 32

Loud and Soft *by Julie Holder* 34

The Echo Bridge *by Daphne Lister* 36

Can You Hear? *by Judith Nicholls* 41

First Steps *by Julie Holder* 43

With My Hand *by John Foster* 44

I Am the Boss *by John Foster* 46

Playthings *by Daphne Lister* 48

Bouncing to the Moon *by Marian Swinger* 50

Here Comes Winter

Hibernating Hedgehog *by Tony Mitton* 52

Bonfire Night *by Irene Yates* 54

At Bimla's House Last Night *by Irene Yates* 56

Winter Walk *by Wendy Larmont* 58

Christmas Eve *by Judith Nicholls* 60

Chinese New Year *by Wendy Larmont* 62

You Can Tell It's Spring *by Charles Thomson and John Foster* 64

Eid Mubarak *by Marian Swinger* 66

Seasons of Trees *by Julie Holder* 68

One Summer Evening *by John Foster* 70

Spiders in the Sandwiches

I Like *by John Foster* 72

I Went to the Fridge *by John Foster* 74

When Susie's Eating Custard *by John Foster* 76

When the Giant Comes to Breakfast *by John Coldwell* 78

Chinese Takeaway *by John Foster* 80

Picnic Tea *by David Harmer* 82

Shopping List *by Julie Holder* 84

Wrong Trolley *by Eric Finney* 86

Whoops! *by Judith Nicholls* 88

Poppadoms *by John Foster* 89

Pancake Day *by John Foster* 90

Glossary 92

Index of first lines 94

Enjoying poetry with your child

I Can Read! Oxford Poetry For 5 Year Olds is the first of three books that offer poems for parents to share and enjoy with their children. These poems are perfect for you to read aloud together with your child as they have strong rhythms, simple rhyme schemes and contain lots of repetition.

Poetry is ideal for younger readers. Your child can enjoy a feeling of success after reading a poem which is only a few pages long. Many young readers find this easier than having to read a longer book. The strong rhythms and rhyme schemes of these poems make them ideal for you and your child to learn by heart and perform. You can also use them as a way of introducing simple literary language, using terms such as verse, rhythm and rhyme. The glossary at the end of the book will help you to explain these terms to your child, which appear in orange throughout these notes.

Poetry is great for children's reading development and is a key part of the National Curriculum. These poems make ideal supplementary reading material for any child who is learning to read, so you can use them alongside story books such as *Read with Biff, Chip and Kipper*. You can simply read and enjoy the poems in this book together, or use the notes and tips to help prepare your child to meet the National Curriculum requirements for poetry, which aim to develop children's ability to:

✓	Learn, recite and perform poems
✓	Listen to, read and discuss a wide range of poems
✓	Recognise simple literary language and use terms such as verse, rhythm and rhyme
✓	Show an understanding of poems while reading aloud through intonation, volume and action.

Tips and Ideas for developing reading skills

Introducing literary language

★ Read **Zoo Dream** (p. 20) to introduce alliteration. Encourage your child to pick out words which start with the same letter or sound, e.g. 'monkeys marching' or 'donkeys dancing'. Talk about other animals that you can see at the zoo and make up some similar phrases about them, using alliteration.

★ Read **The Wuzzy Wasps of Wasperton** (p. 26) and ask your child why they think the poet chose the word 'wuzzy' and called the place 'Wasperton'? Can they find any other words with a 'z' sound in them? Focus on the rhyming words and point out how the 'z' sound is echoed in 'plums', 'comes', 'pears' and 'theirs'. Discuss the warning that is given in the last verse.

★ Explain what a riddle is, then read **Pets** (p. 16). Explain how each pet is described without saying what it is and that each is like a riddle. Which lines tell you that the poet is describing a dog, a cat, a rabbit and a budgerigar? Try to make up a similar verse about another pet such as a gerbil or hamster.

★ Explain that onomatopoeia is when words sound similar to the thing they describe. Read **My Goldfish** (p. 14) together and show your child how they can use their voice to emphasise the word 'bark' by using a barking voice and 'mew' by using a mewing voice. Ask your child what other words from the poem you could emphasise in this way.

TOP TIP! Read the other poems in *My Goldfish is the Perfect Pet* together. Explain terms such as narrator, verse, rhyme and rhythm and help your child to use them correctly when discussing poems.

Recognising rhyme and rhythm

★ While reading **With My Hand** (p. 44) encourage your child to identify words that rhyme. Point out how these make a pattern of rhymes in the verses. Then try to make up another verse together using rhymes such as 'knees/ trees' to create lines like, 'With my hand I can touch my knees, I can swing on trees'.

★ Read **My Machine** (p. 32) and talk about the words that are used. Discuss why certain words such as 'ring' and 'ping' come at the end of the line. Read the poem again and help your child recognise rhymes by pausing at the end of each line so that they can provide a word or two that could complete it.

★ Share **First Steps** (p. 43). Try to bring out the rhythm of this poem by reading alternate lines aloud with your child. Let them start so they read lines 1, 3, 5 and 7 and ask them to think about how to say the final line. Then emphasise the rhythm by chanting it together.

★ Try out ways of reading **Bouncing to the Moon** (p. 50) aloud in order to suggest bouncing, for example, reading it with a very pronounced rhythm.

TOP TIP! Ask your child to find other poems in the book that use rhyming words. Work together to add extra verses or to think up new pairs or sets of rhymes to use in the poem.

Discussing and comparing poems

★ Share **You Can Tell It's Spring** (p. 64). Ask your child which of the four verses they like best and why. Talk about the features of spring that the writers have chosen. Encourage your child to suggest other features of spring that they might have included, such as new grass growing or sunnier days. Then try drafting another verse using their suggestions.

★ Before reading **Hibernating Hedgehog** (p. 52), discuss the title and explain what hibernation is. After you read the poem, ask your child what they notice about the first two lines of each verse and what is different about the final verse. Encourage them to recognise the winter theme by picking out words that relate to cold and winter.

★ Explain that **Eid Mubarak** (p. 66) is a poem about a family celebrating Eid, the Muslim festival at the end of Ramadan. Then explain that **Christmas Eve** (p. 60) is a poem about the night before Christmas. Read them aloud in a voice that conveys the excitement in each poem. Then ask your child what the children in both poems are excited about, for example, presents. Discuss what is different about the poems.

★ Read **Bonfire Night** (p. 54). Discuss how sparklers don't actually scatter stars of gold, but the sparks look like gold stars in the dark. Then share **At Bimla's House Last Night** (p. 56), a poem about the Hindu festival of Diwali. Encourage your child to identify similarities in the poems, such as both being set at night, sparklers and celebration. Then explore the differences, such as one poem asking questions while the other doesn't. Ask your child to look for other differences.

TOP TIP! Children are required by the National Curriculum to identify themes in the poems and stories they read. Share the other poems in *Here Comes Winter*, looking for themes. Do any of the poems have similar themes?

Performing poems

★ Talk about having a takeaway for tea, then read **Chinese Takeaway** (p. 80). Decide which parts of the poem you are going to say and which parts your child is going to say to produce a performance of the poem.

★ Discuss which parts of **When the Giant Comes to Breakfast** (p. 78) could be spoken as if by a giant, for example, 'cornflakes with a spade'. Which other parts could be spoken in a gruff giant's voice? Experiment with performances of the poem in which your child takes the part of the child in the poem and you take the part of the giant.

★ Encourage your child to think about how a poem's narrator is feeling. Read **Wrong Trolley** (p. 86) and discuss whether the child is annoyed or puzzled by Mum's behaviour. Share **Picnic Tea** (p. 82) and look at the illustrations to decide whether the children are amused or disgusted. Create a performance of one of these poems and talk about how they could say the lines. Encourage your child to experiment with different ways of saying the lines to suggest how the narrator feels.

★ Actions and gestures can be part of a performance. While you read **When Susie's Eating Custard** (p. 76), encourage your child to perform the actions. Discuss some other messy foods that Susie could eat, such as raspberries or biscuits, and try to add new verses and actions.

TOP TIP! Encourage your child to learn poems off by heart and to perform and recite them. Let them choose their favourite poem from *Spiders in the Sandwiches* and help them to memorise it, then use actions and intonation to create a performance.

My Goldfish is the Perfect Pet

Look for other poetry collections in the library that you can share with your child, such as **Whizz Bang Orang-utan, See you later, Escalator** *and* **Cockadoodle Moo!** *When you read them, discuss the poems by using literary language such as* simile, alliteration *and* rhythm.

My Goldfish

My goldfish is
    the perfect pet.
She isn't any trouble.
She doesn't bark.
She doesn't mew,
    just bubbles
        bubbles
        bubbles.

My goldfish is
    the perfect pet.
She isn't any trouble.
We don't have
    to feed her much.
She doesn't need
    a rabbit hutch,
        just bubbles
            bubbles
            bubbles.

Marie Brooks

Pets

I have a pet.
He loves a ball.
He likes his food.
He gobbles it all.
He wags his tail
And loves a walk.
He does what I say.
I wish he could talk.

I have a pet
With silky fur.
And after tea
She likes to purr.
She drinks her milk
And eats her fish
From her own little
Dinner dish.

I have a pet.
He lives in a hutch.
He nibbles carrots.
He eats so much!
With long brown ears
And twitching nose,
In and out
Of his hutch he goes.

I have a pet
Who whistles and sings,
With a yellow beak
And bright green wings.
He lives in a cage.
I know what he needs—
Water and sand
And nuts and seeds.

Gwenda Izzet

Zoo Dream

I dreamed I went
to the zoo one day.
All the animals
came out to play.
There were

Ten whales whistling,
Nine hippos hopping,
Eight monkeys marching,
Seven lions laughing,

Six snakes skipping,
Five donkeys dancing,
Four crocodiles clapping,

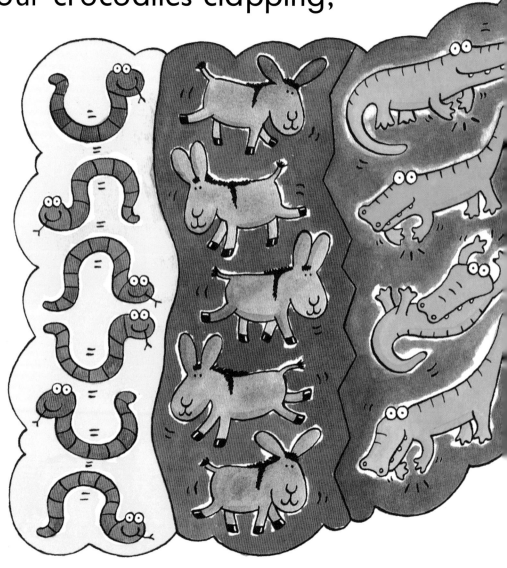

Three rhinos roaring,
Two giraffes giggling,
And one seal snoring!

John Foster

In My Garden

In my garden,
My pets are free.
Sometimes they come
To play with me—
Butterflies, all kinds of bugs,
Ladybirds and snails and slugs,
Caterpillars and bumblebees,
Which live among the grass and trees.

Gwenda Izzet

The Wuzzy Wasps of Wasperton

The wuzzy wasps of Wasperton
Are buzzing around the plums
And sucking all the juicy ones
Before somebody comes.

The wuzzy wasps of Wasperton
Are buzzing around the pears
And choosing all the ripest ones—
They think the orchard's theirs.

The wuzzy wasps of Wasperton
Steal fruit fit for a king.
But don't disburb them if you go—
Those wuzzy wasps can STING!

Daphne Lister

My Pet Giraffe

I'm sure you would laugh
At my pet giraffe.
He really stands out in a crowd.
For he's the only pet
I've taken to the vet
After bumping his head on a cloud.

John Coldwell

Ting!
Went the Triangle

Play rhyming games, such as **rhyme** *tennis, in which you and your child take it in turns to think of rhyming words. For example, you start with the word 'ball', your child replies 'wall' and you go on exchanging words until one of you is stuck. The other person wins a point. You can use a rhyming dictionary such as the* **Oxford First Rhyming Dictionary** *to help you.*

My Big Band

'Ting' went the triangle.
'Foo' went the flute.
'Whee' went the whistle.
The horn went 'Toot'.

'Crash' went the cymbal.
'Boom' went the drum.
'Ta-ra' went the trumpet.
'Quiet!' yelled Mum.

Tony Mitton

My Machine

It's got knobs you can twiddle,
And bells you can ring,
It's got parts you can waggle,
And things you can ping.

It's got levers you pull,
It's got wheels that whizz round,
And what does it make?
Just a wonderful sound!

Richard James

33

Loud and Soft

YOU MUST SHOUT
IF I'M FAR AWAY
SO I CAN HEAR
WHAT YOU WANT TO SAY.

But if you and I
Are near,
You can whisper
And I will hear.

Julie Holder

The Echo Bridge

There's an old bridge
Where I sometimes go,
If I stand underneath it
And shout, 'Hello!'

'Hello, hello, hello,'
I hear the call.
Yet there's no one else there –
Just me, that's all.

I roar like a lion,
And one roars back,
I howl like a wolf,
And I hear the whole pack.

I growl like a tiger,
And more growls come,
It feels so scary –
I run back home to Mum.

Daphne Lister

Can You Hear?

The wind is a giant's breath.
I can hear him under my door.
He puffs and pants.
He moans and groans.
He whistles across my floor.

Judith Nicholls

First Steps

One step, two steps,
The baby toddles.
Three steps, four steps,
The baby wobbles.
Five steps, six steps,
The baby falls flat.
My mum says I used to do that.

Julie Holder

43

With My Hand

With my hand I can turn on a tap,
I can give you a clap,
I can scratch my nose,
I can tickle my toes.

With my hand I can scoop up sand,
I can hold your hand,
I can point to the sky,
I can wave goodbye!

John Foster

I Am the Boss

I am the boss.
What I say goes.
Clap your hands
And touch your toes.

I am the boss.
Look over here.
Waggle your thumbs
And scratch your ear.

I am the boss.
Jump like a clown.
Bend your knees
And all sit down!

John Foster

Playthings

Can you bounce, bounce, bounce
like a big, bouncy ball,
trying to look over
the garden wall?

Can you float, float, float
like a bright balloon,
sailing through the air
on its way to the moon?

Daphne Lister

Bouncing to the Moon

We're on a bouncy castle.
We'll be jumping off it soon,
unless you pull the plug out
and we whizz off to the moon.

Marian Swinger

Here Comes Winter

*Remind your child of favourite nursery rhymes or songs and enjoy sharing or making up nonsense versions such as **Twinkle Twinkle Chocolate Bar**. Type or write out your creations for your child to illustrate and make a book.*

Hibernating Hedgehog

Here comes winter,
cold and grey.
The hedgehog tucks
itself away.

Here comes ice
and here comes snow.
It needs somewhere
warm to go.

Here comes mist
and freezing fog.
Here's a good old
hollow log.

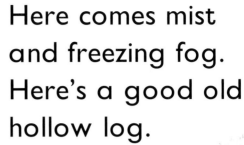

And here's a pile
of leaves that's deep.
It rolls up tight
and goes to sleep.

Tony Mitton

Bonfire Night

In the night-time darkness,
In the night-time cold,
Did you spot a Catherine wheel
Raining showers of gold?
Did you watch a rocket
Go zoom and into the sky?
And hear the bonfire crackle
As the sparks lit up the guy?
In the night-time darkness,
In the night-time cold,
Did you clutch a sparkler
As it scattered stars of gold?

Irene Yates

At Bimla's House Last Night

At Bimla's house last night
We had fireworks and
Sparklers and rice and
Sweet, juicy
Jum-jums bigger than
Gobstoppers.

At Bimla's house last night
Her dad lit up
All the rooms with candles,
And down in the kitchen
Her mum was so pleased
She gave me a hug.
At Bimla's house last night
We all sang
Songs and wished each other

Happy Diwali!

Irene Yates

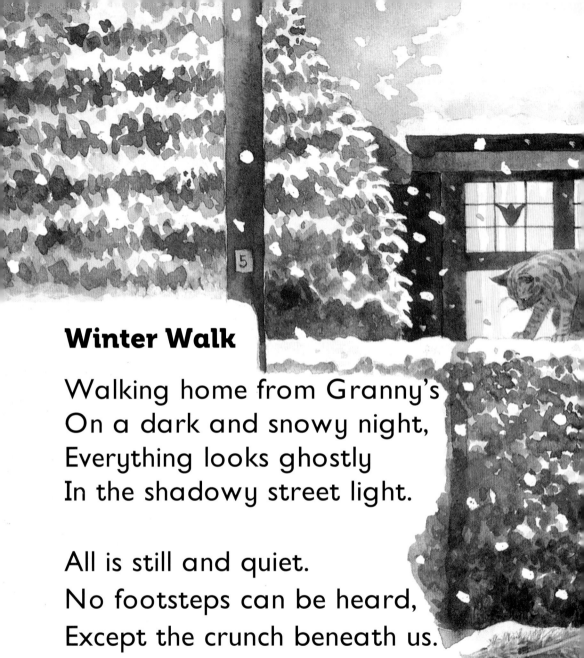

Winter Walk

Walking home from Granny's
On a dark and snowy night,
Everything looks ghostly
In the shadowy street light.

All is still and quiet.
No footsteps can be heard,
Except the crunch beneath us.
Too cold to say a word.

Wendy Larmont

Christmas Eve

Nearly midnight;
still can't sleep!
Has he been yet?
Dare I peep?

Sneak out softly,
creaking floor!
Down the stairs
and through the door…
In the darkness
by the tree,
tightly wrapped…
but which for me?

Feel the ribbon,
find the card!
This one? That one?
Heart thumps hard.
Trembling fingers,
throbbing head,
then ...

a voice yells,

'BACK TO BED!'

Judith Nicholls

61

Chinese New Year

Dragons, lions,
Red and gold.
In with the new year,
Out with the old.

Banners flying,
Bands playing.
Lion prancing,
Dragon swaying.

Fireworks cracking,
Lanterns swinging.
People laughing,
Dancing, singing.

Dragons, lions,
Red and gold.
In with the new year,
Out with the old.

Wendy Larmont

You Can Tell It's Spring

You can tell it's spring
When the trees turn green
And there are just puddles
Where the snow has been.

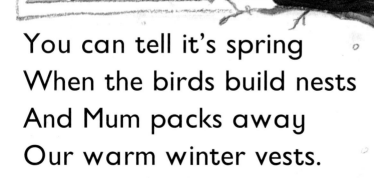

You can tell it's spring
When the birds build nests
And Mum packs away
Our warm winter vests.

You can tell it's spring
When the yellow heads
Of daffodils dance
In the flower beds.

You can tell it's spring.
It's lighter each day,
And after school
We can stay out and play.

Charles Thomson and John Foster

Eid Mubarak

There's Granny, Uncle, Aunty,
my cousins at the back.
They're hugging Mum and Daddy.
We cry, 'Eid Mubarak.'
We've had lots of cards
and presents,
there's a knocking at the door.
Can it be my Grandad
bringing us some more?
Yes, it's really Grandad.
What's that behind his back?
We hug him in the hallway
and shout, 'Eid Mubarak.'

Marian Swinger

Seasons of Trees

In spring
The trees
Are a beautiful sight
Dressed in blossom
Pink and white.

In summer
The trees
Are full of treats
Apples and pears
And cherries to eat.

In autumn
The trees
Are red and gold
And the leaves fall down
As the days grow cold.

In winter
The trees
Are bare and plain,
Waiting for spring
To dress them again.

Julie Holder

69

One Summer Evening

We were playing cricket
in the garden after school.
Dad dived for the catch,
but he missed
and fell in the paddling pool!

John Foster

Spiders in the Sandwiches

Look out for clues in poems that can provide ideas about how to perform them. For example, you could look for examples of **onomatopoeia**, or words that describe a setting or mood (such as 'dark', 'snowy' or 'cold') or words that describe sounds and actions.

I Like

I like sizzling sausages.
I like bubbling beans.
I like mashed potatoes
With gravy and greens.

I like cold ice cream.
I like chocolate cakes.
But most of all I like
The jellies my mum makes.

John Foster

I Went to the Fridge

I went to the fridge.
I opened the door.
There on the shelves
Inside I saw
    Ten fish fingers
    Nine strawberry yoghurts
    Eight beefburgers
    Seven slices of ham
    Six large eggs
    Five cold sausages
    Four chunks of cheese
    Three bottles of milk
    Two cans of Coke
    And a big bowl of blackcurrant jelly.

John Foster

When Susie's Eating Custard

When Susie's eating custard,
It splashes everywhere—
Down her bib, up her nose,
All over her high chair.

She pokes it with her fingers.
She spreads it on her hair.
When Susie's eating custard,
She gets it everywhere.

John Foster

When the Giant Comes to Breakfa[st]

When the giant comes to breakfast
He eats cornflakes with a spade,
Followed by a lorry load
Of toast and marmalade.
Next, he takes a dustbin,
Fills it up with tea,
Drinks it all in a gulp,
And leaves the mess for me.

John Coldwell

Chinese Takeaway

What would you like for supper, today?
Shall we go out and get a takeaway?

Beef chop suey with egg fried rice,
Sweet and sour chicken
– that sounds nice!

Crisp crunchy bean sprouts,
mushrooms and peas.
Shall we get a takeaway?
Shall we eat Chinese?

Ooh, Mum, can we?
Ooh, yes, please!

John Foster

Picnic Tea

We found a shady spot under a tree.
Here's what we had for a picnic tea.

We had ants in the sandwiches,
       wasps in the jam,
       slugs in the lettuce leaves,
       beetles in the ham,
       midges in the orange juice,
       flies on the cheese,
       spiders on the sausages,
       ice cream full of bees!

David Harmer

Shopping List

We went to the baker's
For bread and for buns.

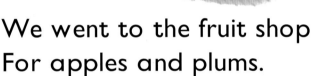

We went to the fruit shop
For apples and plums.

We went to the butcher's
For sausage and ham.

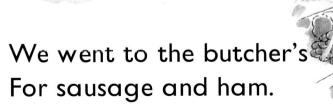

We when to the grocer's
For butter and jam.

We went to the newsagent
For a comic for me.

Then we went to the café
For orange juice and tea.

Julie Holder

Wrong Trolley

Mum, there's cat food in our trolley,
And we haven't got a cat!
There's a big bag of potatoes,
And we didn't load up that.
Do you remember loading beans
Or peas or cauliflower?
Mum, I know we're pushing it
But is this trolley ours?

Eric Finney

Whoops!

Our supermarket keeps baked beans
inside a plastic bin.
They used to pile them on the floor,
till James picked up the BOTTOM tin!

Judith Nicholls

Poppadoms

Poppadoms, poppadoms,
  plain or full of spice.
Poppadoms, poppadoms,
  with chicken and rice.
Crispy hot poppadoms
  to crunch and chew.
A plateful of poppadoms
  just for me and you.

John Foster

Pancake Day

It's Pancake Day!
It's Pancake Day!
Hurry home to tea!
There'll be pancakes for you!
There'll be pancakes for me!

Dad's cooking pancakes
In the frying pan,
Turning them by tossing them
As high as he can.

It's Pancake Day!
It's Pancake Day!
Sit down for your tea.
There are pancakes for you!
There are pancakes for me!

Dad's made some pancakes,
Crisp and golden brown.
Sprinkle them with sugar
And gobble them down!

John Foster

Glossary

alliteration the use of several words which begin with the same letter or sound, e.g. slip, slop, slap

emphasise to put stress on a word or words

intonation varying the pitch of your voice, making it rise or fall in order to convey emotion or meaning

narrator the person or character who is telling a story

onomatopoeia the use of a word or phrase which has a sound that echoes its meaning, e.g. hiss, buzz, clatter

rhyme words which end with the same sound or sounds are said to make a rhyme

rhyme scheme the pattern of rhymes in a poem

rhythm the flow of words or phrases in a poem, based on the number and type of syllables they have

riddle a word puzzle in which you write about something without saying what it is, so that the reader must use the clues to figure it out

simile comparing one thing with another by using 'like' or 'as', e.g. 'as big as an elephant'

theme the subject of a poem, or an idea such as friendship or celebration which runs throughout the poem

verse a section of a poem, often with the same rhyme scheme as other sections

Index of First Lines

At Bimla's house last night 56

Can you bounce, bounce, bounce 48

Dragons, lions, ... 62

Here comes winter, ... 52

I am the boss. 46

I dreamed I went 20

I have a pet. 16

I like sizzling sausages. 72

I went to the fridge. 74

I'm sure you would laugh 28

In my garden, ... 24

In spring 68

In the night-time darkness, ... 54

It's got knobs you can twiddle, ... 32

It's Pancake Day! 90

Mum, there's cat food in our trolley, ... 86

My goldfish is 14

Nearly midnight; 60

One step, two steps, ... 43

Our supermarket keeps baked beans 88

Poppadoms, poppadoms, ... 89

The wind is a giant's breath. 41

The wuzzy wasps of Wasperton 26

There's an old bridge 36

There's Granny, Uncle, Aunty, ... 66

'Ting' went the triangle. 30

Walking home from Granny's 58

We found a shady spot under a tree. 82

We went to the baker's 84

We were playing cricket 70

We're on a bouncy castle. 50

What would you like for supper, today? 80

When Susie's eating custard, ... 76

When the giant comes to breakfast 78

With my hand I can turn on a tap, ... 44

You can tell it's spring 64

YOU MUST SHOUT 34